The Nature Kid's Guide to NARWHALS

DAVID ANDERSON

LP Media Inc. Publishing
Text copyright © 2026 by LP Media Inc.
All rights reserved.

For information address LP Media Inc. Publishing,
30012 Variolite St NW, Princeton MN 55371
www.lpmedia.org

Publication Data

Narwhals
The Nature Kid's Guide to Narwhals — First edition.

Summary: "Learn all about Narwhals, the Nature Kid Way"
— Provided by publisher.

ISBN: 979-8-89818-138-3

[1. Narwhals – Non-Fiction] I. Title.

Title: The Nature Kid's Guide to Narwhals

CONTENTS

ICY WATERS

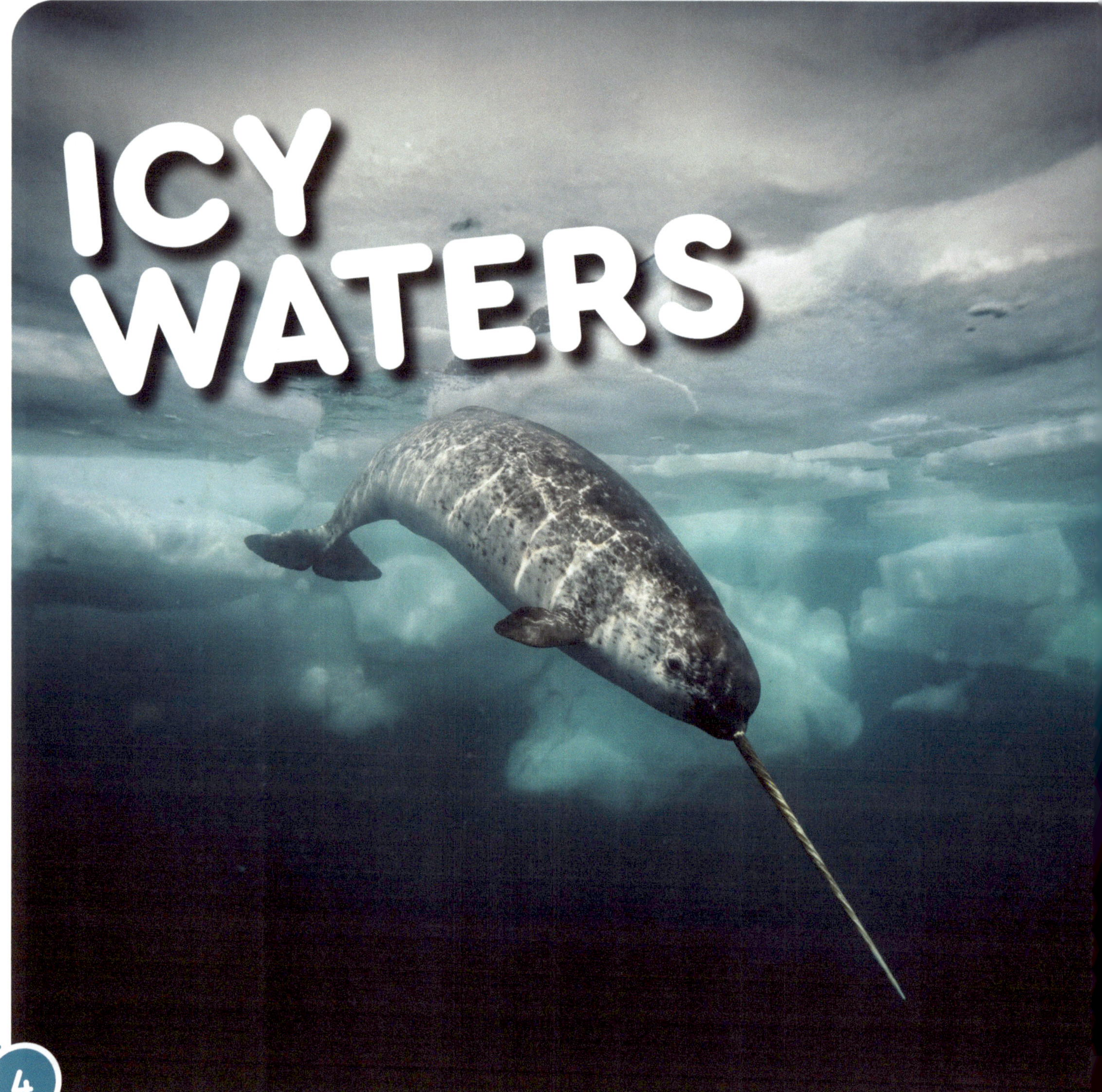

Splash! A narwhal dives deep under thick Arctic ice.

Narwhals live in the coldest seas on Earth. They swim in the Arctic Ocean all year long, surrounded by big chunks of floating ice.

These whales love dark, icy water. They stay close to ice packs and frozen bays. The water is so cold it would sting your skin!

A narwhal is right at home in this frozen world. Its body is made for the cold. Thick **blubber** keeps it warm even in freezing water. What a tough animal!

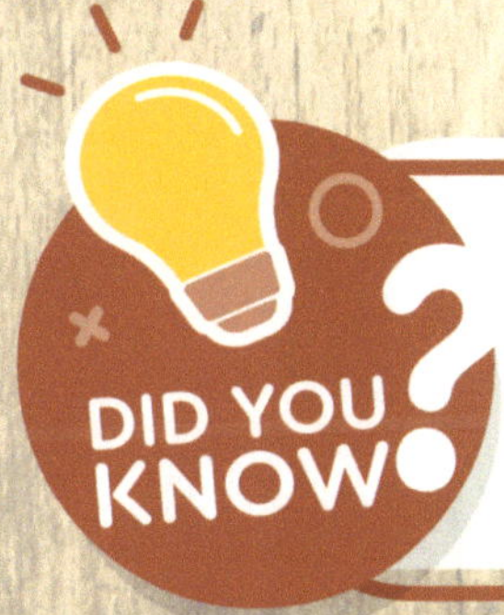

Narwhals can live for more than 50 years — some scientists think a few reach 100!

ARCTIC
AREAS

Whoosh! Cold Arctic winds blow over a pod of narwhals.

Canada and Greenland are home to most narwhals. Some swim near Norway and Russia too. Most stay in the far, far north.

In summer, they move to shallow bays near shore. When winter comes, they head to deep, open water. They follow the ice as it shifts each year.

These icy waters are perfect for narwhals. Plenty of food and lots of ice — no wonder so many call it home!

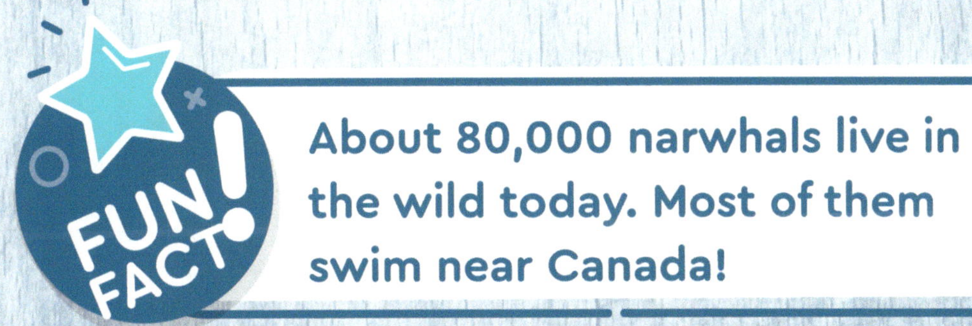

About 80,000 narwhals live in the wild today. Most of them swim near Canada!

SIZE UP

Narwhals and beluga whales
are cousins — the only two
members of their whale family!

Whoa! A narwhal glides by, almost as long as a car!

Narwhals are medium-sized whales, but do not let that fool you. A grown male can stretch to 16 feet long and weigh 3,500 pounds. That is as heavy as a small truck!

Males are bigger than females and carry most of that weight in their thick, round bodies. All that bulk is packed with blubber, which keeps them warm in some of the coldest water on Earth.

Their smooth, tapered shape helps them slice through icy Arctic water with ease. Narwhals are built for speed, cold, and deep dives into the dark ocean below.

TWISTED TUSKS

Swoosh! A long spiral tusk rises out of the cold waves.

The narwhal's tusk is really a tooth! This long tooth grows right through the upper lip. It can reach up to ten feet long.

Most male narwhals grow a tusk. The tooth always twists to the left as it gets longer. It looks like a long, spiraling horn.

The tusk is hollow inside. It is not hard like a rock — it can bend a tiny bit without breaking. Pretty cool for a tooth!

A few female narwhals grow tusks too, but theirs are much shorter and thinner.

SOUND SCAN

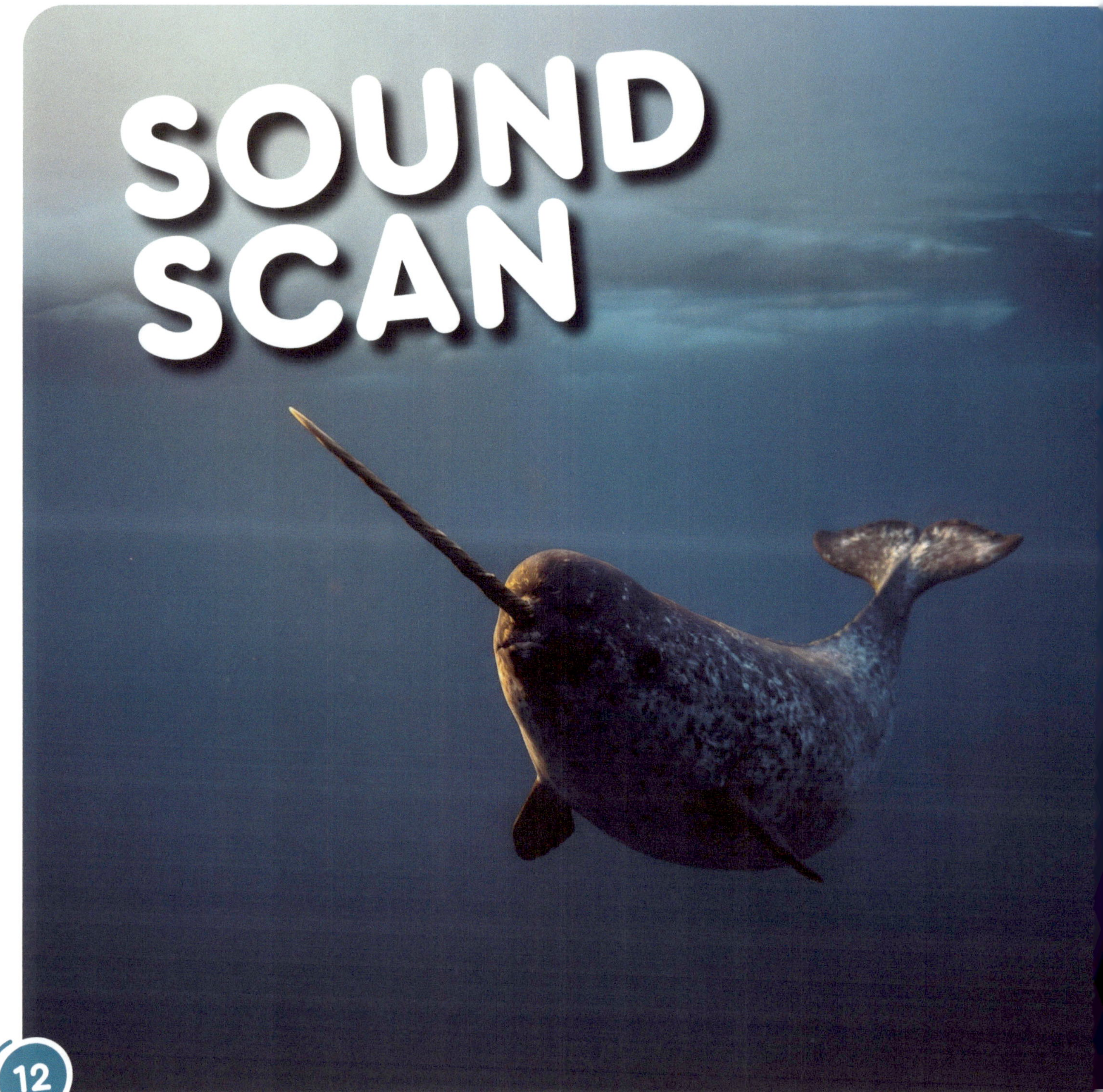

Click, click, click! A narwhal sends sounds into the deep.

Narwhals use sound to find their way. They make clicks that travel through dark water. The clicks bounce off things and come back.

This is called **echolocation**. It helps narwhals find food in the deep, dark sea. It also helps them find gaps in the ice above.

A fatty lump on the narwhal's head sends out the clicks. This lump is called a melon. It works like a built-in speaker!

A narwhal's tusk has millions of tiny nerve endings — it can sense water temperature and saltiness!

STAY SAFE

Shhh! A narwhal's dark skin helps it hide in the deep sea.

Narwhals do not have many ways to fight. No sharp claws. No teeth for biting. Their best trick is to hide or swim away fast.

Their skin helps them hide in the water. Dark backs blend with the deep sea below. Light bellies blend with the bright sky above.

This sneaky coloring tricks predators. It makes narwhals harder to spot from above and below. Even big whales can be hard to find!

Narwhals have been swimming in Arctic waters for over 5 million years!

A hungry narwhal can eat up to 60 pounds of food in a single day — that is like eating 240 fish sticks!

Gulp! A full narwhal comes back up after feeding in the deep.

Narwhals eat fish, squid, and shrimp. Arctic cod and Greenland halibut are two of their favorites, swimming in the cold dark water right below the ice where narwhals spend most of their time.

Narwhals do not chew their food. They suck it in whole using a powerful suction from their small mouths. What they lack in teeth they make up for in speed!

In winter they eat more than in summer. They need extra food to stay warm and keep their thick layer of blubber full. A stuffed belly is what gets them through the coldest, darkest months of the year.

DEEP DIVES

Whoosh! A narwhal plunges straight down into the dark deep.

Narwhals are amazing divers. They can dive more than 5,000 feet deep — almost a mile straight down!

They hunt near the ocean floor. Down there, it is pitch black and freezing cold. Narwhals use their clicks to find prey in the darkness.

A deep dive can last about 25 minutes. Then they swim back up to breathe. Narwhals may dive 15 to 20 times each day just to find food.

A narwhal's heart slows from 60 beats per minute to just 10 during a deep dive!

KILLER
CHASERS

DID YOU KNOW?

Orcas sometimes trap narwhals in shallow bays, circling them before attacking!

Swoosh! A pod of orcas cuts through the Arctic water on the hunt.

Orcas are the biggest threat to narwhals. These large hunters chase narwhals in open water. A group of orcas can catch even a fast-swimming narwhal.

Polar bears hunt narwhals too. They wait by cracks in the ice. When a narwhal comes up to breathe — the bear strikes!

Some sharks may also attack narwhals. But orcas and polar bears are the main dangers. Life in the **Arctic** can be risky.

QUICK ESCAPE

Narwhals make special whistles and clicks to warn their pod when danger is near.

Zoom! A narwhal races away from danger at top speed.

When danger is near, narwhals move fast. They can hit 15 miles per hour in short bursts, which is surprisingly quick for such a large, round animal. A scared narwhal does not waste any time!

Narwhals also dive deep under thick sea ice to hide. Orcas are powerful hunters but too large to follow them into the narrow channels beneath the ice. The frozen ceiling above becomes a perfect shield.

Sometimes a whole pod flees together at once, swimming in a tight group and moving as one coordinated unit. In the Arctic Ocean, staying together is often what keeps them alive.

SWIM STRONG

A narwhal's tail flukes can stretch more than three feet wide — as long as a baseball bat!

Swish! A narwhal's tail pumps up and down through the water.

Narwhals swim by moving their tails up and down. Their wide, flat tail **flukes** push them through the water. This gives them lots of power.

They have two small flippers on their sides. These help them steer and turn. But here is something odd — narwhals have no fin on their backs!

Having no back fin helps in icy water. A fin could bump and scrape the ice above. Without one, narwhals glide smoothly under the icy ceiling.

DAILY LIFE

Narwhals sometimes float at the surface with their tusks poking straight up like unicorn horns!

Blub, blub! A narwhal pops up to take a breath of fresh air.

Narwhals spend most of their day looking for food. They dive, eat, and come back up to breathe. Then they do it all again!

Between meals, narwhals rest near the surface. They float and breathe slowly. These quiet breaks give their bodies time to recover.

Narwhals are active day and night. In the Arctic summer, the sun can shine for 24 hours straight. In winter, it stays dark for weeks. Narwhals keep swimming through it all.

POD PALS

Male narwhals and female narwhals often travel in separate pods until mating season!

Squeak! A narwhal calls out to its pod in the cold water.

A group of narwhals is called a pod. Pods can have 10 to 20 whales in them. They swim, eat, and travel together.

In summer, many pods come together. Hundreds of narwhals gather in the same bay — sometimes over a thousand! It is like a big whale party.

Narwhals in a pod look out for each other. They share feeding spots and watch for danger. Being in a group helps everyone survive.

TUSK BATTLES
FUN FACT!
A very small number of male narwhals grow two tusks instead of one!
30

Clack! Two male narwhals cross their tusks above the waves.

Male narwhals use their tusks to compete for mates. They rise to the surface and raise their tusks up into the air, crossing and rubbing them together. This is called tusking.

Tusking does not usually cause harm. The males push and cross tusks gently. It helps them show how big and strong they are.

Females pick the males with the longest tusks. A big tusk means the male is healthy and strong. Mating happens in the spring, under the ice.

CUTE CALVES
DID YOU KNOW?
A narwhal mom carries her baby for about 15 months — 6 months longer than a human pregnancy!

Swish! A newborn narwhal calf swims up for its very first breath.

Baby narwhals are called **calves**. They are born in the summer months. A calf comes out tail first into the cold water.

Newborn calves are about five feet long — as tall as an adult person! They are dark gray all over. They can swim right away, but they stay very close to mom.

A mother narwhal has just one calf at a time. Twins are very rare. Each calf is special and gets all of mom's care.

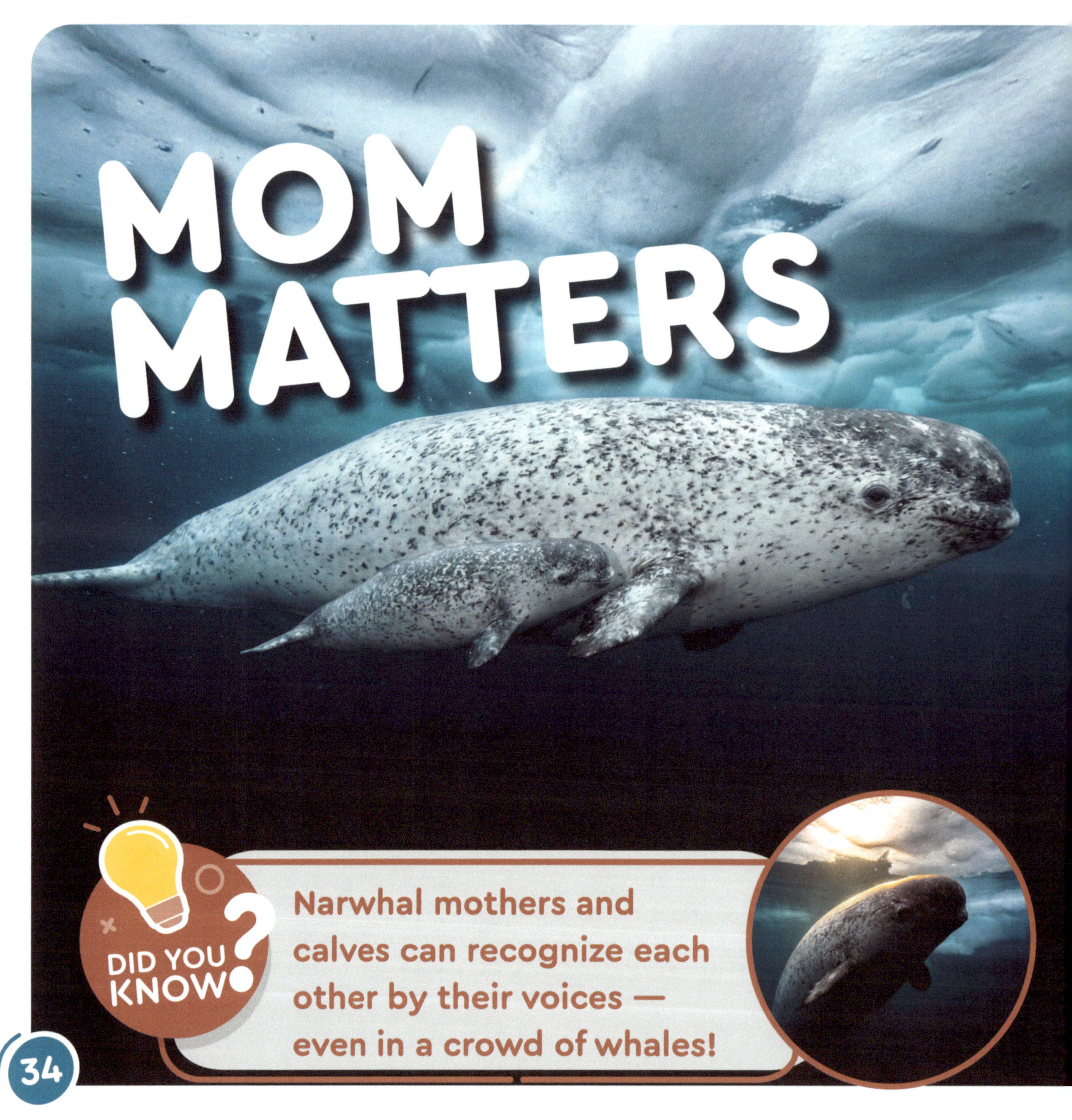

Narwhal mothers and calves can recognize each other by their voices — even in a crowd of whales!

Swoosh! A narwhal mother and her calf glide together through the icy Arctic water.

Mother narwhals take great care of their calves. They feed them rich, fatty milk. This milk helps the baby grow a thick layer of blubber fast.

A calf drinks its mother's milk for about 20 months. That is more than a year and a half! All that milk makes the calf strong.

Moms swim close to their calves at all times. They keep them safe from cold and danger. A narwhal mom is always on watch, always ready to protect her baby.

MELTING ICE

DID YOU KNOW?
The Arctic is warming about twice as fast as the rest of the world — ice that took thousands of years to form is disappearing!

Drip! Arctic ice melts faster and faster every single year.

The Arctic is warming up fast. Sea ice is melting more each year. This is a big problem for narwhals.

Less ice changes everything. It means less cover and fewer places to rest. Warmer water may push their favorite fish away to colder spots.

Noise from big ships and oil drills bothers them too. The loud sounds can scare narwhals away from feeding spots. People need to help keep the Arctic safe and quiet.

HELP OUT

Inuit people in the Arctic have lived alongside narwhals for over 4,000 years — and still help protect them today!

Hooray! People around the world are helping save narwhals!

Scientists study narwhals to learn how to help them. They track pods with small tags. This shows where narwhals go and what they need to survive.

Some areas of the ocean are now protected. Ships must slow down or stay away. This keeps the water quiet and safe for narwhals.

Kids can help too! Learning about narwhals is a great first step. Saving energy at home helps keep the Arctic cold. Every little bit matters for these amazing unicorns of the sea.

GLOSSARY

Arctic

The very cold area around
the North Pole

blubber

A thick layer of fat under a
whale's skin

calves

Baby narwhals

echolocation

Using sounds to find
things in the dark

flukes

The flat, wide parts at the
end of a whale's tail